Bridge-Logos
Gainesville, Florida USA

Bridge-Logos
Gainesville, FL 32614 USA

04   1

Library of Congress Catalog Card Number: pending
International Standard Book Number 0-88270-790-6

for Rowena,
beautiful child of God,
who has an angelic capacity
for loving unlovable creatures

...with special acknowledgment
of life-long indebtedness to
Elena

...and in loving memory of
Tex

THE PLAYERS

Theodore "THEO" Knox

Cerebral, studious, and absolutely devoted to Jesus.
Loves: reading the Bible, arguing with unbelievers, staying up
all night making thousand-word points on internet
message boards, coffee
The Low-Down: Theo is sensitive, tactful, and very left-brained.
Tends toward a cautious and over-intellectual Gospel
presentation. (This is where Lunk sets him off best.)
Pre-Salvation: He was a clever, somewhat obnoxious atheist;
often got beaten up, usually after winning rigged bets.

Intriguing out-of-context quote:
"Should a gift Bible
be accompanied by
a chimp in a bikini?"

Pete "LUNK" Lunkinopoulos

Big, zealous ball of unbridled enthusiasm for Jesus.
Loves: reading the Bible, eating out after church, off-the-cuff
chatroom "discussions," corndogs
The Low-Down: Lunk is eccentric, tactless, and very right-brained.
In actuality, he's a genius, though he may come across as simply
in need of medication. (Theo understands him, sort of.)
Pre-Salvation: He was a shy loner and horoscope fanatic,
planning to become a mad scientist and take over
the world with a cyborg army.

Intriguing Out-of-Context Quote:
"Tomorrow you're in Haiti
dripping chicken blood
on frog innards!"

FRANKLE

(Rhymes with "ankle." As far as anyone
knows, this is his full name.)

Resident atheist/evolutionist.

Loves: standing around contemplating life's utter meaninglessness,
sniping at Christians, candy bars, Theo and Lunk's company ... secretly

The Low-Down: Frankle is contentious and venomous, but harmless. He often
fares rather poorly in arguments with Theo and Lunk. (He does get some good
jabs in on occasion, but his overall lack of skill at masking the inherent
weaknesses of his preferred worldview, compared with the average devoted
atheist/evolutionist, is notable -- and is directly attributable to
the biases of the cartoonist.)

YEAH. i'D DO
MUCH BETTER
iN THE HANDS
OF A SMART
GUY!

Intriguing out-of-context quote:
"In your dreams, freaks."

The Occasional Cult Member

Usually Mormons (generally because they're
easy to pick on -- not simply due to their sort of
"comic strip friendly" theology, but also because they
comprise the majority of the cartoonist's in-laws.)
Provide good "truth in love" practice
for Theo and Lunk.

Sterling

Alley-dwelling composite character.
Any resemblance to any one person
is not intended. He's supposed to
resemble a whole lot of people
at the same time.

Rather Unpleasant Older Women

For some reason, whenever an older lady
appears, she's almost guaranteed to be of the
crabby variety. The cartoonist, who finds most
older ladies very sweet and likable, apologizes
for this phenomenon.

Pastor Phil

The Warrior Guys' beloved "teacher" is never
actually drawn in the strip. This is sort of an homage
to the greatest comic strip of all time. Don't think
that this is simply because the artist is a
slacker. It's mostly the homage thing.

Author's Explanatory Note on Evolution

This compilation book features Warrior Guys strips dating back to the very first ones created – more than 385 million years ago, when soda-pop was only a nickel and nobody cussed on TV. However, the strips are not chronologically ordered. Therefore, you may occasionally note that, for example, Lunk is suddenly a little "long in the tooth" or his head looks enormous (more enormous than usual, I mean), or Frankle looks like Frankle's cousin at best. Please try not to let this impede your enjoyment of the book. The characters' appearances have reached equilibrium, I assure you. No significant further mutation will take place, as should be clearly demonstrated by their comparatively consistent looks in future Warrior Guys compilations (unless, of course, some new ferocious predator character is introduced, the presence of which would naturally force Theo and Lunk to sprout wings).

LUNKOPITHECUS   THEO HABILIS   ATHEIST MAN

Theo & Lunk

Warrior Guys

By
Dustin Runyan

i JUST WATCHED THE EVENING NEWS.

YEAH? THAT'S ALWAYS DEPRESSING.

JESUS iS COMING BACK ANY DAY NOW.

OH, MAN! THEY FiNALLY REPORT SOMETHING GOOD AND i MiSS iT!

HAVE YOU SEEN MY KiNG JAMES VERSION?

NOPE.

MY 'NEW KiNG JAMES' VERSION?

NUH-UH.

HOW ABOUT MY 'REViSED AMERICAN DOUBLE-STANDARD LiViNG STUDY BIBLE FOR LEFT-HANDED BUNGEE-JUMPERS'?

WHAT?

JUST SEEiNG iF YOU WERE PAYiNG ATTENTION.

GiMME YOUR MONEY!

SORRY, WE DON'T FEAR DEATH - ONLY THE LORD.

NOTHING PERSONAL.

i'M REALLY POOR AND i NEED SOME MONEY?

OOO! DRAT!

HE'S SMARTER THAN HE LOOKS.

1

4

i KNOW ATHEISTS DON'T LIKE TO HEAR THIS, FRANKLE, BUT i PRAY FOR YOU ALMOST EVERY DAY.

YEAH? GUESS YOU MISSED LAST TUESDAY!

A BIG, STUPID BILLBOARD BLEW OVER ON TOP OF ME AND MY BICYCLE!

HEY! THAT'S THE DAY i PRAYED FOR GOD TO GIVE YOU A SIGN!

BEAUTIFUL.

"...AND HE WILL DIRECT THY PATHS"... "HE WILL DIRECT THY PATHS..."

WHAT ARE YOU DOING?

ACKNOWLEDGING GOD "IN ALL MY WAYS", ALA PROVERBS 3:6

WOW-- EVEN IN THE WAY YOU ROLL DICE. IMPRESSIVE.

HA! SEVEN! YOUR PATH JUST GOT DIRECTED TO BOARDWALK, BUDDY!! WOOO-HOO!!

"All things work together for good..."

PAY UP, BIBLE SCHOLAR BOY!!...

HERE YOU GO, SIR! iT EXPLAINS HOW THE TRUE BIBLE SAYS WE MUST WORSHIP COFFEE!

AND CALL iT BY iTS COOLEST NAME!

UMM... UH.. ACTUALLY...

BYE-BYE!

WHO WAS THAT?

OH, JUST SOME JAVA'S WITNESSES.

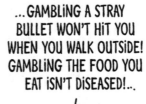

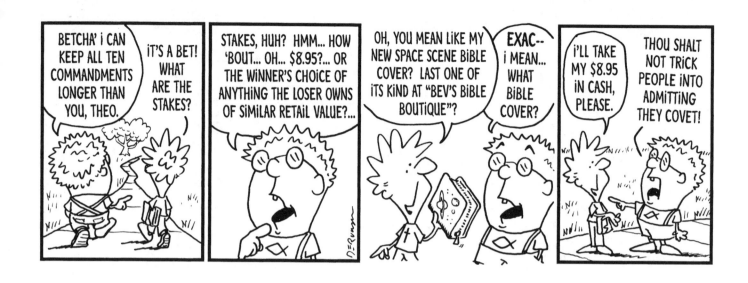

Warrior Guys ...of the Round Table

15

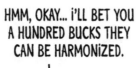

YEAH, I KNOW WHAT WE TALKED ABOUT...

BUT THERE'S A FINE LINE BETWEEN RESPECTING THE NATIVES' CUSTOMS AND... I DON'T KNOW...

...THAT.

HEY - WHEN IN ROME...

HEY, FRANKLE, DID YOU KNOW THAT GOD SO LOVED THE WORLD THAT HE G--

PREACH TO THE HAND.

HEY, FRANKLE'S HAND, DID YOU KNOW THAT GOD SO LOVED THE WORLD THAT HE G--

ON SECOND THOUGHT, THE LAST THING I NEED IS A SAVED HAND.

SEEMS STRANGE THAT NOAH WOULD BOTHER LOADING BUGS ONTO THE ARK.

WELL, I'D THINK THE ARTHROPODS WERE MAINLY JUST STOWAWAYS.

OH, YOU MEAN, LIKE, THE FLEAS AND TICKS SNUCK IN ON THE DOGS? AND THE SPIDERS IN THE HAY?...

YEAH.

...AND THE ROACHES IN MRS. NOAH'S FAMOUS CRUNCHY FIG SALAD?...

YES. EXACTLY, LUNK.

23

...AND **THAT**, MY FRIEND, IS THE SCIENTIFIC PROOF FOR MACRO-EVOLUTION!

UMM, ACTUALLY THAT'S NOT "PROOF".

THAT'S SIMPLY AN INTERPRETATION OF A CHOICE SUBGROUP OF THE FACTS, OFFERED AS DEBATABLE SUPPORT FOR A FOREGONE CONCLUSION.

THAT IS -- AS OPPOSED TO SOUND SCIENCE, WHICH DRAWS CONCLUSIONS BASED ON, AND NEVER IN CONFLICT WITH, THE ENTIRETY OF AVAILABLE DATA -- YOU, LIKE MOST EVOLUTIONISTS, ARE MERELY INTERPRETING SELECT DATA IN SUCH A WAY AS BEST "PROVES" YOUR ALREADY DECIDED BELIEF, DISMISSING INTERPRETATIONS OF EQUAL OR GREATER HOLISTIC VALIDITY, DUE SOLELY TO THEIR NON-SUPPORT OF THE THEORY.

HEY -- STOP MESSING WITH MY FOREGONE CONCLUSION THAT CHRISTIANS ARE STUPID.

SORRY.

CAN I HAVE ANOTHER FORK, PLEASE? THIS ONE HAS A BENT PRONG-THINGY.

SURE.

WAIT -- ON SECOND THOUGHT, I'LL KEEP IT.

WE'D BE IN REAL TROUBLE IF GOD JUST REPLACED **US** WHENEVER HE SAW AN IMPERFECTION!

DON'T YOU WORRY, LITTLE GUY! I WILL IN NO WISE CAST YOU OUT!

HE REALLY NEEDS A PET.

HMM... THIS GUY'S OKAY.

I THOUGHT YOU HATED T.V. PREACHERS.

I NEVER SAID I "HATED" 'EM... I JUST DON'T LOVE 'EM LIKE YOU DO. SOME ARE FINE.

I NEVER SAID I "LOVED" 'EM... SOME AREN'T SO GREAT.

DID WE JUST KIND OF AGREE ABOUT T.V. PREACHERS?

THIS MUST BE THE MIRACLE I SENT IN MONEY FOR!!...

i JUST SAW A NEWS REPORT ABOUT PEOPLE WHO ARE SUiNG FAST FOOD PLACES FOR MAKING THEM UNHEALTHY.

AND iT WAS REPORTED WiTH A BiAS THAT MADE ME ALMOST SYMPATHETiC WiTH THE PLAiNTiFFS.

WOW. THAT'S DiSTURBiNG.

i'M GONNA SUE THE NEWS FOR MAKING ME STUPiD.

AH, THE iNFAMOUS WiNDMiLL HOLE!

OR, AS i LiKE TO CALL iT, THE 'VALLEY OF THE SHADOW OF DEATH' HOLE...

...BELiEViNG, AS i DO, THAT MiNiATURE GOLF iS A PERFECT METAPHOR FOR A LiFE iN CHRiST.

WHiCH iS A BiT SiLLY.

HOLE-iN-ONE! TAKE THAT, DEATH! WOOF! WOOF!

OF COURSE, THE METAPHOR DOES HAVE iTS MOMENTS.

LET ME GUESS -- YOU SEE THIS HOLE AS A METAPHOR FOR THE TRIBULATION.

CLOSE...

i CALL iT THE "PASTOR SEARCH" HOLE.

I'VE BEEN THINKING ABOUT THE RICH YOUNG RULER...

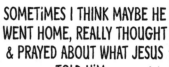

SOMETIMES I THINK MAYBE HE WENT HOME, REALLY THOUGHT & PRAYED ABOUT WHAT JESUS TOLD HIM...

...AND THEN GOD CHANGED HIS HEART, AND HE GAVE AWAY ALL HE HAD AND FOLLOWED JESUS AFTER ALL.

WOW. COOL THOUGHT.

SOMETIMES I THINK MAYBE HE LOOKED LIKE ADAM SANDLER.

COUPLE OF DEEP THINKERS WE ARE.

i'M GONNA GRILL SOME HOT DOGS. HOW MANY YA' WANT?

ONE, i GUESS.

JUST ONE?!

i'D LOVE HOT DOGS, BUT i CAN'T HELP THiNKING OF WHAT THEY'RE MADE OF.

HMM.

i LOVE HOT DOGS UNCONDITIONALLY.

YOU'RE A BETTER MAN THAN i.

"OH, MAN! THIS ISN'T ANY FUN! HEY --CAN LAZARUS BRING ME SOMETHING TO DRINK?"

"NO WAY, RICH MAN! YOU'VE GOT SOME NERVE, YOU KNOW THAT?! DON'T YOU KNOW WHERE YOU ARE?

"WELL, AT LEAST LET ME GO BACK AND TELL THE GUYS AT THE YACHT CLUB..." "NO WAY, RICH MAN!"

OH. Hi.

YOU'RE A WEIRD GUY, LUNK.

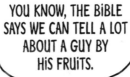

EVERY TOOTHPASTE CLAIMS TO BE "WHITENING" THESE DAYS.

IT'S A LIE, I TELL YA! A FILTHY LIE!

YOUR TOOTHPASTE CAN'T SAVE YOU, MA'AM!!

WELL, I'M SURE WE'LL BE SEEING HER IN CHURCH SUNDAY...

GET THEE BEHIND ME, MINTY FRESH SATAN!

WHAT ARE YOU DOING IN THE GREETING CARD SECTION?

IT'S STERLING'S BIRTHDAY. I'M GIVING HIM A GIFT BIBLE. I JUST NEED THE RIGHT CARD.

THIS IS A NICE ONE, HUH?

HMM. YEAH.

BUT SHOULD A GIFT BIBLE BE ACCOMPANIED BY A CHIMP IN A BIKINI?

GOOD POINT. I'LL GET HIM THE CHIMP IN A ONE-PIECE.

HELLO, MA'AM... I COULDN'T HELP NOTICING SOME OF THE SMUTTY ARTICLES THAT MAGAZINE IN YOUR BASKET FEATURES. HOPE YOU'RE NOT PLANNING ON READING THOSE.

HMM... THIS ONE ABOUT J-LO'S NEW HAIR-DO SEEMS WHOLESOME ENOUGH...

30

SO, FRANKLE TELLS ME YOU ACTUALLY HIT HIM OVER THE HEAD WITH THE BIBLE YESTERDAY.

YEP!

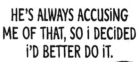

HE'S ALWAYS ACCUSING ME OF THAT, SO i DECIDED i'D BETTER DO iT.

THAT'S TERRIBLE.

NO, iT'S GREAT! FROM NOW ON, WHENEVER HE SAYS iT, HE WON'T BE BEARING FALSE WITNESS!

i MADE FRANKLE A LESS SINFUL PERSON!

YOU'VE REALLY THOUGHT ABOUT THIS, HAVEN'T YOU?

BELiEVE, FRANKLE!

iS THAT iT? "BELiEVE, FRANKLE?" COME ON, YOU CAN DO BETTER THAN THAT.

BELiEVE, FRANKLE!

WHOP!

i CAN'T BELiEVE YOU HiT FRANKLE OVER THE HEAD WiTH YOUR BiBLE AGAiN.

HEY, JUST TRYING SOMETHING NEW.

LUNK, WE CAN'T RESORT TO ViOLENCE iN EVANGELiSM.

AW, COME ON-- THE LUNKiSH iNQUiSiTiON iS JUST GETTiN' STARTED!

GiMME THE THUMB-SCREW, LUNK...

32

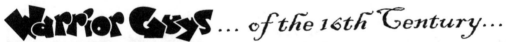

33

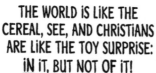

35

37

Warrior Guys ...of middle-earth

40

41

44

HEY, FRANKLE. EVER THINK ABOUT THE FACT THAT IN ORDER FOR ANYTHING AT ALL TO EXIST...

...SOMETHING -- I'M NOT SAYING WHAT -- HAS TO POSSESS THE INCOMPREHENSIBLE QUALITY OF INDEPENDENT SELF-EXISTENCE?...

...AND THAT THERE HAS TO HAVE BEEN AN INCOMPREHENSIBLE "BEFORE TIME" STATE -- AN "ETERNITY", IF YOU WILL -- IN ORDER FOR TIME AS WE KNOW IT TO HAVE POSSIBLY BEGUN?

I TRY NOT TO. WHY?

OH, JUST CURIOUS.

I'M JUST THINKIN' -- ONCE YOU FACE THE FACT THAT REALITY DOES INCLUDE AT LEAST ONE COMPONENT THAT'S HOPELESSLY INCOMPREHENSIBLE TO THE HUMAN MIND...

...THAT IS, THE "TIMELESS AND SELF-EXISTENT" COMPONENT...

...THEN YOU'RE LEFT WITH NO GROUNDS EXCEPT PURE FAITH FOR REJECTING THE EXISTENCE OF GOD... RIGHT?

DUH!

WHY DO YOU THINK I NEVER FACE THAT FACT?! NOW, LET'S CHANGE THE SUBJECT ALREADY!...

CORNDOG?

YOU SEE - THE ONLY THING WE CAN COMPREHEND ABOUT "TIMELESSNESS" AND "SELF-EXISTENCE" IS THE FACT THAT THEY ARE NECESSARY FOR THE EXISTENCE OF... WELL... EXISTENCE.

BUT WE CAN'T POSSIBLY COMPREHEND THOSE TWO QUALITIES THEMSELVES.

I THOUGHT WE WERE GONNA TALK ABOUT CORNDOGS.

YEAH, COME ON, MR. THEOLOGY PANTS! LET'S SAY GRACE!

DANG! iT CRASHED AGAIN!

TODAY, COMPUTERS CRASH. 3,000 YEARS AGO, SiCKELS BROKE AND OXEN WENT LAME.

No, No, Please No...

AS SOLOMON WROTE: "THERE'S NOTHING NEW UNDER THE SUN."

i BET SOLOMON NEVER GOT HiS HiGH SCORE ON 'BATTLE TOADS' ERASED.

ALL iS VANiTY, DUDE. DEAL WiTH iT.

T.V.'S JUST A BiG SiN-FEST ANYMORE.

YEP. HERE A SiN, THERE A SiN.

EVERYWHERE A SiN SiN.

'OLD MacDONALD HAD A T.V.'?

i'LL GET THE GUiTAR, YOU GET THE TAPE RECORDER!

THiS iS GONNA BE HUGE!

WOW. WRiTiNG A GOOD CHRiSTiAN SONG FOR PRE-SCHOOL AGE KiDS iS HARDER THAN YOU'D THiNK...

SO FAR WE'VE GOT 'OLD MacDONALD HAD A T.V., E-i-E-i-O', PLUS THE 'EVERYWHERE A SiN SiN' PART, AND THEN WE'RE KiNDA STUCK.

HMM... MAYBE GOD'S PLAN iSN'T FOR US TO BE RiCH AND FAMOUS CHRiSTiAN RECORDING ARTiSTS AFTER ALL.

HEY! HOW ARE WE EVER GONNA BE RiCH AND FAMOUS CHRiSTiAN RECORDING ARTiSTS WiTH THAT ATTiTUDE?!

SORRY.

YOU CREATIONISTS AND YOUR "CATASTROPHISM"!

THERE'S NOTHING LESS SCIENTIFICALLY VALID THAN THE NOTION THAT MAJOR GLOBAL EVENTS CAUSING SIGNIFICANT CHANGES OVER VERY SHORT TIME PERIODS, MAKING SCIENCE'S STANDARD AGE CALCULATION METHODS UNRELIABLE, MAY HAVE OCCURRED!

WAIT... THAT SOUNDED TOO SCIENTIFICALLY VALID...

YOU BETTER WORK ON THAT.

I'M APPLYING FOR THAT NURSERY WORKER SPOT AT CHURCH.

COOL... THEY MIGHT BE WANTING A WOMAN, THOUGH.

ALREADY THOUGHT OF THAT...

I ALLAY THEIR FEARS OF A MALE IN PARAGRAPH TWO, SENTENCE THREE.

"I WILL NOT TEACH THE KIDS HOW TO MAKE ARMPIT NOISES."

I'M ALSO GONNA MENTION I'LL BATHE...

I CAN'T BELIEVE YOU SENT 20 DOLLARS TO **THAT** T.V. PREACHER. HE'S A "GIVE-TO-GET" GUY!...

...I GUESS NOW YOU'RE EXPECTING A BIG BAG OF MONEY TO FALL OUT OF THE SKY, RIGHT?

OH, PLEASE! I'M NOT STUPID!

I'M THINKING MAYBE A METEORITE -- I HEAR THOSE ARE WORTH BIG BUCKS!

48

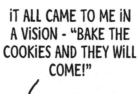

49

52

53

 YOU DON'T MIND BEING THE SUBJECT OF A LITTLE STUDY, DO YOU, THEO?

STUDY?

 I'M TESTING THE "COINCIDENCE THEORY" OF JESUS' FULFILLMENT OF OLD TESTAMENT MESSIANIC PROPHECIES...

 IF JESUS' LIFE JUST HAPPENED TO HAVE FULFILLED THEM, THEN IT STANDS TO REASON THAT THE AVERAGE PERSON'S LIFE WILL ALSO.

 SO, UM, YOU'LL BE DOING THIS 'TIL I DIE?

QUESTION #1: HAVE YOU EVER NOTICED ANYONE CASTING LOTS FOR YOUR CLOTHING?

 WELL, THEO, ANOTHER DAY HAS PASSED WITHOUT YOU FULFILLING A SINGLE MESSIANIC PROPHECY.

BUMMER.

 ONCE AGAIN YOU DIDN'T MAKE ANY BLIND PEOPLE SEE, ONCE AGAIN NO ONE BETRAYED YOU FOR THIRTY PIECES OF SILVER...

 ONCE AGAIN I WASN'T BORN IN BETHLEHEM.

I DON'T KNOW HOW YOU'RE GONNA PULL THAT ONE OFF, DUDE.

 OKAY, MY STUDY'S ALL DONE.

ALREADY, HUH?

 YEP. HERE ARE THE FINDINGS I'LL BE SUBMITTING TO THE "JOURNAL OF SCHOLARLY BIBLICAL RESEARCH STUFF".

COOL.

"CONCLUSION: THEO'S A NICE ENOUGH GUY, BUT YOU COULDN'T MISTAKE HIM FOR THE MESSIAH EVEN IF YOU WANTED TO."

 I MUST ADMIT I'M SOMEWHAT RELIEVED.

HERE'S A CONSOLATION SUCKER.

WAIT A SEC. THIS CREDIT CARD SAYS I'M PRE-APPROVED...

...BUT I HAVE TO APPLY ANYWAY?

THAT'S LIKE THE LORD SAYING, "YOU'RE SAVED, UNLESS YOU CAN'T PROVE YOU DESERVE IT"!

AND ANYONE WHO'D COMPARE SALVATION TO A CREDIT CARD--

DOESN'T DESERVE IT! MY POINT EXACTLY!

CHRISTIANS NEED TO BEAR EACH OTHER'S BURDENS, RIGHT?

UH...

HERE - HIT YOUR THUMB WITH THIS HAMMER.

I'D FEEL MUCH BETTER IF MY BROTHER IN CHRIST WERE GOING THROUGH THIS AGONY WITH ME.

HOW ABOUT I JUST PRAY FOR YOUR THUMB?

THAT'LL WORK. OH, AND PRAY FOR MY LANGUAGE WHILE YOU'RE AT IT...

THERE'S A NEW STUDY THAT PROVES DISCIPLINING CHILDREN IS BAD FOR 'EM.

I THOUGHT THE NEW STUDY PROVED IT'S GOOD FOR 'EM.

NO, YOU'RE THINKING OF THIS MORNING'S PAPER.

THIS IS THE EVENING EDITION.

BOY, IT'S HARD TO KEEP UP WITH THE SMART PEOPLE.

DANG, WHY DID THEY HAVE TO CATCH FRANKLE'S POP FLY?

IF WE HAD WON -- ON FRANKLE'S HIT, OF ALL THINGS -- WHAT A MIRACLE! HE'D HAVE TO BELIEVE IN GOD NOW!

WELL, I DUNNO -- I THINK HE MIGHT HAVE ACTUALLY DIED FROM THE SHOCK.

LIKE I SAY -- HE'D HAVE TO BELIEVE IN GOD NOW!

NOW THAT'S JUST MEAN, LUNK.

HIGHLIGHTER PENS ARE SO HANDY!

YEAH.

KIND OF DEFEATS THE PURPOSE TO HIGHLIGHT THE WHOLE BIBLE, THOUGH.

I DON'T WANNA HIGHLIGHT OUT OF CONTEXT!

WANNA GO THROW THE FOOTBALL? I ALWAYS GOTTA' PLAY FOOTBALL AFTER I WATCH IT.

WELL, MAYBE LATER. I'M STUDYING THE SODOM AND GOMORRAH ACCOUNT. PRETTY FASCINATING STUFF.

WANNA GO THROW FIRECRACKERS ON AN ANT BED?

AH, THE ONION RING! NO BEGINNING, NO END...

...HELPING TO FIX OUR MINDS ON THE TIMELESS THINGS OF THE HEAVENLY REALM.

THANK YOU, MY LITTLE BATTER-DIPPED GLIMPSE OF ETERNITY!

SORRY, TATER TOT. YOU'RE GOOD WITH KETCHUP. THAT'S ABOUT IT.

OH, MAN...

I HATE WHEN THAT HAPPENS. I JUST SPLATTERED A GNAT ON MY BIBLE.

OOO, RIGHT ON 1 SAMUEL 17:50.

THAT'S A LITTLE IRONIC.

IT DID TURN OUT BETTER FOR GOLIATH THAT TIME.

I THINK FRANKLE HAS A DEMON OF UNBELIEF.

REALLY? I THINK HE DISBELIEVES ALL BY HIMSELF.

LEAVE ME ALONE OR I'M SPEWIN' PEA SOUP ON BOTH OF YA'!!

I DO THINK HE HAS A DEMON OF SNIPPINESS.

WELL... GUESS WE'RE ALMOST DONE WITH MRS. NEWBY'S LAWN.

YEP.

SO, UH - MAYBE WE SHOULD TALK WITH HER. I'M NOT SURE SHE'S A CHRISTIAN.

WHAT DO YOU MEAN? SHE'S GOT THAT "SMILE! GOD LOVES YOU!" BUMPER STICKER.

OH, YEAH. GEE, WHAT WAS I THINKING.

...AND I'M PRETTY SURE SHE WATCHES "TOUCHED BY AN ANGEL"...

HI, MRS. NEWBY. FINISHED YOUR LAWNWORK... NOPE - NO CHARGE.

I AM WONDERING IF YOU COULD SETTLE A BET, THOUGH.

I THINK YOU'RE GOING TO HEAVEN, THEO HERE THINKS YOU'RE GOING TO HELL-

SLAM!

HMM... MAYBE 'GOOD COP, BAD COP' ISN'T THE BEST EVANGELISM TECHNIQUE.

YA THINK?!!

HELLO, MA'AM. CAN WE TALK FOR A MINUTE ABOUT ETERNITY...? UH, MA'AM?...

...YOUR LIFE IS LIKE ONE OF THOSE EGGS IN YOUR BAG, MA'AM! ONE DAY YOU'LL JUST GO SPLAT, AND IF YOU DON'T HAVE JESUS--

SPLAT!
SPLAT!
SPLAT!

SHE HAD TWINKIES IN THAT BAG, TOO, YA KNOW.

OH, UH - EXCUSE ME MA'AM! YOUR LIFE IS ALSO LIKE A TWINKIE!...

63

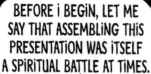

WELL, i DiD iT, THEO!

!

i BARGED RIGHT INTO THAT ADULT BOOK STORE AND STARTED TELLING EVERYONE ABOUT JESUS!

WOW -- THAT TOOK SOME GUTS! i KNEW YOU'D GET PUNCHED.

i DIDN'T GET PUNCHED.

i RAN INTO A SHELF. YOU DON'T THINK MY EYES WERE UNDERLINE OPEN, DO YA'?

SIR, iF YOU DIED TODAY, HOW SURE ARE YOU THAT Y-- STOP RIGHT THERE!

JUST GET AWAY FROM ME, YOU FREAKS! i KNOW YOUR TYPE! LEAVE ME ALONE OR i'LL SMACK YA!

WOW... WELL, JESUS PROMISED WE'D BE PERSECUTED FOR HiS NAME'S SAKE...

DANG INSURANCE SALESMEN!

BUS STOP

UH-OH... i KNOW THAT WOLF-WHISTLE.

iT BETTER NOT BE FOLLOWED BY THE SMELL OF--

UGGH!
cough!
cough!

LUNK! YOU JUST READ iSAiAH 52:7 AGAIN, DIDN'T YOU?!

WOO-WOO! GET A LOAD A' THEM BEAUTIES!

68

Warrior Guys ...of the Martial Arts Flicks

WELL, CRAZY AL, LUNK AND I HAVE TALKED IT OVER, AND WE'VE DECIDED NOT TO GO WITH JIHAD PEST CONTROL.

WE'VE CONCLUDED THAT YOUR METHODS ARE HIGHLY INEFFICIENT.

YEAH. AND DUMB, TOO.

IN THE LONG RUN ALL YOU'D DO IS MAKE OUR ROACHES ANGRY, MORE DETERMINED, AND STRONGER THAN EVER!

NOT TO MENTION SUSPICIOUS.

WE'LL HAVE NO RACIAL PROFILING AMONG OUR ROACHES!

STILL WORKIN' THE RELIGION MESSAGE BOARDS, HUH?

YEP.

DO YOU REALLY THINK PEOPLE TAKE THE TIME TO READ THOSE HUGE POSTS OF YOURS?

WELL... NOT EVERYONE SHARES YOUR TASTE IN WEB COMMUNICATION. WHAT'S THAT CALLED AGAIN?...

..."INSTANT MESSAGING SMILEYS"?

HEY -- THAT "ABOUT TO BARF" FACE IS WORTH A THOUSAND WORDS!

DEAR LORD -- LET ME KNOW IF THIS IS THE RIGHT MESSAGE FOR THIS BUDDHISM BOARD... SHOULD I CHANGE IT?... ADD STUFF?... DELETE STUFF?...

...AND IT'S 3 A.M.!... THESE GUYS'LL SEE THAT, AND THEY MIGHT THINK I'M AN OBSESSIVE FREAK... SHOULD I... POST IT... NOW?...

click!

"THANK YOU FOR POSTING AT DEEP-DISCUSSIONS.COM!"

GUESS THAT'S A YES.

74

Warrior Guys *...of Acts 9:33-34*

FRANKLE SEEMS EXTRA DOWN TODAY.

HMM.

MAYBE THE DARK, UTTER HOPELESSNESS OF HIS ATHEISTIC EXISTENCE IS FINALLY STARTING TO GET TO HIM.

HA! YOU WISH!

FOR YOUR INFORMATION, I'M PERFECTLY HAPPY WITH THE DARK, UTTER HOPELESSNESS OF MY ATHEISTIC EXISTENCE!

"...IN JESUS' NAME, AMEN."

"...IN JESUS' NAME, AMEN."

COOL! WE GOT STERLING TO SAY THE "SINNER'S PRAYER"!

YEP. AND YOU KNOW WHAT THEY SAY...

...SIXTEENTH TIME'S A CHARM.

I'M PRETTY SURE HE MEANT IT THAT TIME!

BURP.

HMM... EVER WONDER ABOUT SAYING GRACE IN PUBLIC, LIKE WE JUST DID? YOU KNOW, CONSIDERING MATTHEW 6:6?

WELL, WE DON'T DO IT TO IMPRESS PEOPLE.

TRUE.

ISN'T IT COOL HOW I KNEW THAT VERSE? AM I AWESOME OR WHAT?!

AMAZING.

79

THANK YOU! THANK YOU! IT'S GREAT TO BE SINGING PRAISES TO JESUS HERE AT SILVER HILLS NURSING HOME!

Clap. Clap. Clap. Clap.

WE ACTUALLY WEREN'T PLANNING ON BEING HERE, BUT, WELL... AMAZING HOW THE LORD CAN GUIDE YOUR STEPS SOMETIMES...

CAREFUL, LUNK. THEY'RE EATING.

...HOW CAN I PUT IT? UM... LET'S JUST SAY, THIS WAS NO DREAM, AND I KNEW EXACTLY WHOSE FOOTPRINT IT WAS...

...WON'T LET SATAN *fff!* IT OUT -- I'M GONNA LET IT SHINE! LET IT SHINE! LET IT SHINE! LET IT SHIIINE!

Clap. Clap. Clap.

THANK YOU! WHAT AN AUDIENCE!

Silver Hills NURSING HOME

SO, HOW MANY LITTLE LIGHTS ARE SHININ' BRIGHT TONIGHT? SHOW OF HANDS?...

NONE!? COME ON, PEOPLE! JOHN WROTE REVELATION WHEN HE WAS, LIKE, A HUNDRED! WHAT'S THE PROBLEM?!

oh, man, oh, man...

WAIT, I GOT A THEORY -- HOW MANY OF YOU WOULD RATHER BE BANISHED TO THE ISLAND OF PATMOS THAN LIVE HERE?...

WELL, THE NURSING HOME WAS A GOOD WARM-UP... I'M PUMPED NOW! LET'S GO DO SOME STREET PREACHING!

YOU SURE? ROUGHER CROWD, YA' KNOW.

OH, I WOULDN'T SAY THAT.

I'VE NEVER BEEN BEANED WITH A SALISBURY STEAK IN THE STREET.

WOW. THAT THING LEFT A WELT...

81

IS THIS LEPROSY?

I DON'T WANNA HAVE TO LIVE OUTSIDE THE TOWN LIMITS! TELL ME IT ISN'T LEPROSY!

UMM... IT'S DRIED MASHED POTATO.

WHEW!

WAIT -- DOES THAT MAKE ME CLEAN OR UNCLEAN?

I THINK IT JUST MAKES YOU A SLOB.

THANK YOU.

DON'T THANK ME, MA'AM -- THANK JESUS!

IF IT HAD JUST BEEN ME, I'D HAVE LET THAT DOOR SLAM RIGHT BACK IN YOUR FACE!

BECAUSE I'D HAVE BEEN TOO BUSY PLOTTING THE NEXT SELFISH THING I WANTED TO DO WITH MY ROTTEN, GODLESS EXISTENCE!

TRULY, IT WAS NOT I WHO HELD THAT DOOR, BUT CHRIST WITHIN ME!

THAT'S HIS WAY OF SAYING "YOU'RE WELCOME," MA'AM.

OH. OKAY.

HA! "JAZZ"! 31 POINT WORD ON A TRIPLE WORD SPACE! 93 POINTS, BABY!! GO, LUNK! GO, LUNK!...

UMM... THAT'S A HAND-WRITTEN "10", AND A DAB OF PEANUT BUTTER COVERING THE ORIGINAL NUMBER.

I'VE DONE NOTHING WRONG! THE RULES DON'T SPECIFI-CALLY FORBID MAKING A "Z" TILE OUT OF AN "N" TILE!

I'LL GIVE YOU 3 POINTS FOR THE DECENT PHARISEE IMPRESSION.

I'LL TAKE IT!

...NAH, WE'RE NOT NEW TO THE AREA. LUNK AND i JUST THOUGHT iT MiGHT BE A NiCE CHANGE OF PACE TO ViSiT A DiFFERENT CHURCH TODAY.

WELL, YOU GUYS CAME TO THE RiGHT PLACE! THiS iS THE BEST PRESBYTERiAN CHURCH iN THE TRi-COUNTY AREA... HANDS DOWN!

...then sings my SOOOOUL, my Savior...

COOL.

NO, REALLY, LUNK-- HANDS DOWN! YOU'LL FREAK EVERYONE OUT!

i'M iN A DiLEMMA... i DON'T FEEL QUiTE RiGHT ABOUT GETTiNG ALL iNTO HALLOWEEN, YA' KNOW?

ON THE OTHER HAND, THERE'S NO OTHER DAY WHEN YOU CAN GO AROUND ASKiNG STRANGERS FOR FREE CANDY AND ACTUALLY GET iT.

WELL... YOU COULD CALL iT "BEGGAR'S DAY" AND DRESS LiKE LAZARUS.

AND YELL, "TREAT OR ETERNAL DAMNATiON!" BRiLLiANT!

ACTUALLY, CHRiSTiANS DO HAVE GREAT REASON TO CELEBRATE ON HALLOWEEN.

OCTOBER 31ST iS "REFORMATiON DAY"....

...THE BEGiNNiNG OF THE CHURCH'S COURAGEOUS, HiSTORiC STRUGGLE AGAiNST THE BLASPHEMOUS ABUSES AND CRUEL TYRANNY OF ROME.

WOW. iF THAT AiN'T CAUSE FOR FREE MALTED MiLK BALLS i DUNNO WHAT iS!

87

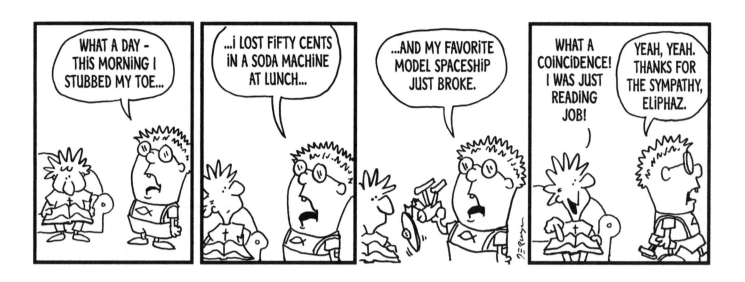

Warrior Guys ..of the Final Frontier

"Come to Me, all who
are weary and heavy
laden, and I will give
you rest."

Matt. 11:28